The Boy,
the mole,
the fox
and the Horse.

This book is dedicated
to my lovely kind mum,
and my wonderful dog
Dill.

THE BOY, THE MOLE, THE FOX AND THE HORSE

Charlie Mackesy

Hello

You started at the beginning, which is impressive. I usually start in the middle, and never read introductions. It's surprising that I've made a book because I'm not good at reading them. The truth is I need pictures, they are like islands, places to get to in a sea of words.

This book is for everyone, whether you are eighty or eight — I feel like I'm both sometimes. I'd like it to be one you can dip into anywhere, anytime. Start in the middle, if you like. Scribble on it, crease the corners and leave it well thumbed.

The drawings are mainly of a boy, a
mole, a fox and a horse. I'll tell you
a little bit about them - although
I'm sure you'll see things here that I
don't, so I'll be quick.

   The boy is lonely when the mole
first surfaces. They spend time together
gazing into the wild. I think the wild
is a bit like life - frightening sometimes
but beautiful.

   In their wanderings they meet the
fox. It's never going to be easy
meeting a fox if you're a mole.

   The boy is full of questions,
the mole is greedy for cake. The
fox is mainly silent and wary
because he's been hurt by
   life.

The horse is the biggest thing
they have ever encountered, and also
the gentlest.
    They are all different, like us,
and each has their own weaknesses.
I can see myself in all four of
them, perhaps you can too.

    Their adventures happen in
Springtime where one moment
snow is falling and the sun
shines the next, which is also
a little bit like life - it can turn
on a sixpence.

I hope this book encourages you, perhaps, to live courageously with more kindness for yourself and for others. And to ask for help when you need it - which is always a brave thing to do.

When I was making the book I often wondered, who on earth am I to be doing this? But as the horse says:

"the truth is everyone is winging it."

So I say spread your wings and follow your dreams - this book is one of mine. I hope you enjoy it and much love to you.

Thankyou. Charlie X

"I'm so small," said the mole.

"Yes," said the boy, "but you make a huge difference."

"What do you want to be when you grow up?"

"Kind" said the boy

"What do you think
success is?" asked the boy

"To love," said the
mole

"Well hello"

"Do you have a favourite
saying?" asked the boy.
"Yes" said the mole
"What is it?"
"If at   first you don't
succeed,   have some cake."
"I see,   does it work?"

"Every time."

"Just a tiny taste"

"I got you a delicious cake," said the mole.
"Did you?"
"Yes"
"Where is it?"
"I ate it," said the mole.
"Oh."
"But I got you another."
"Did you? Where is that one?"
"The same thing seems to have happened."

"What do you think is
the biggest waste of time?"

"Comparing yourself to others,"
said the mole.

"I wonder if there is a school of unlearning"

"Most of the old moles
I know wish they had
listened less to their fears and
more to their dreams."

"What is that over there?"

"It's the wild," said the mole
"Don't fear it."

" Imagine how we would be
if we were less afraid."

"I'm not afraid,"
said the mole.

"If I wasn't caught in this snare
I'd kill you," said the fox.

"If you stay in that snare you will die," said the mole.

So the mole chewed through the wire with his tiny teeth.

"One of our
greatest freedoms
is how we
react to
things"

"I've learned how to be
in the present."
"How?" asked the boy
"I find a quiet spot and
shut my eyes and breathe."

"That's good, and then?"
"Then I focus."
"What do you focus on?"
"Cake," said the mole.

"Isn't it odd. We can only see our outsides, but nearly everything happens on the inside."

"Be careful not to fa..."

...ll "

"So much beauty we need
to look after."

"Being kind to yourself is one of the greatest kindnesses," said the mole.

"We often wait for kindness...
but being kind to yourself can
start now." said the Mole.

"Often the hardest person to forgive is yourself"

"Sometimes I feel lost,"
said the boy.

"Me too," said the mole,
"but we love you, and
love brings you home."

" I think everyone is just
trying to get home,"
said the Mole.

"hello"

"Doing nothing with friends is never doing nothing, is it?" asked the boy

"No," said the mole.

"You fell – but I've got you"

"Everyone is a bit scared,"
said the horse.

"But we are less scared
together."

"Tears fall for a reason and they are your strength not weakness"

" What is the bravest thing
You've ever said?" asked
the boy.

"Help", said the horse.

"When have you been at your strongest?" asked the boy.

"When I have dared to show my weakness."

"Asking for help isn't giving up," said the horse.

"It's refusing to give up."

"Sometimes I worry
You'll all realise
I'm ordinary" said
the boy.

"love doesn't need
you to be extraordinary,"
said the mole.

"We all need a reason to keep going,"
said the horse. "What's yours?"

"You three," said the fox.

"Getting home," said the boy.

" Cake," said the mole.

"I've discovered something better than cake."

"No you haven't," said the boy.

"I have," replied the mole

"What is it?"

"A hug. It lasts longer."

"Nothing beats kindness," said the horse. "It sits quietly beyond all things."

"Sometimes", said the horse.
"Sometimes what?" asked the boy.
"Sometimes just getting up
and carrying on is
brave and magnificent."

"How do they look so
together and perfect?"
asked the boy

"There's a lot of frantic paddling
going on beneath,"
said the horse

"The greatest illusion",
said the mole,

"is that life should be
perfect"

my dog walked over the drawing – clearly trying to make the point

"Is it the moon?" asked the boy.

"it's a tea cup stain..." said the mole, "and where there's tea there's cake"

Be curious

"Life is difficult -
but you are loved."

"So you know all about me?"
asked the boy
"Yes," said the horse.
"And you still love me?"
"We love you all the more."

"Sometimes I think
you believe in me
more than I do,"
said the boy

"You'll catch up,"
said the horse

"The fox never really speaks,"
whispered the boy.

"No. And it's lovely he is with us."
said the horse.

"To be honest, I often feel
I have nothing interesting to say,"
said the fox.

"Being honest is always interesting,"
said the horse.

"There's something I haven't told you,"
said the horse,
"What's that?" said the boy
"I can fly. but I stopped because
it made other horses jealous."

"Well we love you

whether you can fly or not."

"Is your glass half empty or half full?"
asked the mole.
"I think I'm grateful to have a glass,"
said the boy

"We don't know about tomorrow,"
said the horse, "all we need
to know is that we love each other."

"When the big things feel out of control

... focus on what you love right under your nose."

"This storm will pass."

After the Storm

"We have such a long
way to go." sighed the boy.

"Yes, but look how far
we've come;"
said the horse

"Sometimes I want to say
I love you all," said the
mole, "but I find it difficult."
"Do you?" said the boy.
"Yes, so I say something like
I'm glad we are all here."

"OK," said the boy.

"I'm glad we are all here."
"We are so glad you are here too."

"What's your best
discovery?" asked
the mole.

"That I'm enough as
I am," said the
boy.

"I've realised why we are here,"
whispered the boy.
"For cake?" asked the mole.

"To love," said the boy.
"And be loved," said the horse.

" What do we do when our hearts
hurt?" asked the boy

"We wrap them with friendship,
Shared tears and time, till they
wake hopeful and happy again."

"Do you have any other advice?"
asked the boy

"Don't measure how valuable you
are by the way you are treated,"
said the horse

"Always remember you matter,
You're important and you are loved,
and you bring to this world

things no one else can."

"Home isn't always
a place is it?"

"Thank
You"

The ~~end~~

look how
far we've
come

"Sometimes all you hear about is the hate, but there is more love in this world than you could possibly imagine."

This book is about friendship and I couldn't have made it without my friends. So thank you Matthew, Grace, Bear, Phil, Miranda, Amy, Emma, Scarlett, Charlie, Richard and Helen to name a few, whose conversations and love are so part of these pages. X

Thanks to Colm the brilliant Irishman who helped sew this book together often late into the night.

Thank you to everyone at Penguin; Gail, Joel, Tess, Becky, Lucy, Alice, Rae, Beth, Nat, and especially Laura who so kindly coped with me and my messy drawings.

And thank you so much to you on social media who encouraged me with everything.

Thankyou Sara, Daisy and Christopher for your love and endless cups of tea and to my dogs Dill and Barney X

EBURY
PRESS

FIRST PUBLISHED BY EBURY PRESS IN 2019

23

EBURY PRESS IS AN IMPRINT OF EBURY PUBLISHING,
20 VAUXHALL BRIDGE ROAD,
LONDON SW1V 2SA

EBURY PRESS IS PART OF THE PENGUIN RANDOM HOUSE
GROUP OF COMPANIES WHOSE ADDRESSES CAN BE
FOUND AT GLOBAL.PENGUINRANDOMHOUSE.COM

Penguin
Random House
UK

WWW.PENGUIN.CO.UK

A CIP CATALOGUE RECORD FOR THIS BOOK
IS AVAILABLE FROM THE BRITISH LIBRARY

ISBN 978 1 52910 510 0

COLOUR ORIGINATION BY ALTAIMAGE, LONDON
PRINTED AND BOUND IN ITALY BY L.E.G.O. S.P.A

MIX
Paper from
responsible sources
FSC® C018179

PENGUIN RANDOM HOUSE IS COMMITTED TO A
SUSTAINABLE FUTURE FOR OUR BUSINESS, OUR READERS
AND OUR PLANET. THIS BOOK IS MADE FROM FOREST
STEWARDSHIP COUNCIL® CERTIFIED PAPER.